"*Burning the Ghost Light* is a lyrical production of g
longing, and Conlon's poems radiate in the limeligh
and a gentle humility. I have truly never read a collection like it before; Conlon has brought a level of stunning evolution to not just her own writing but to the craft itself."

— SIERRA DEMULDER, author of *Ephemera*

"Caitlin Conlon has written an innovative and unyielding powerhouse of a book. In *Burning the Ghost Light,* Conlon does what all the best poets do: she slows down each moment and lets the reader savor each ache and awe, life's entrances and exits, to create an emotional landscape so vulnerable, so lived-in, it takes your breath away. From grocery lists to thrift store receipts to deleted scenes, Conlon engineers strange and surprising forms to examine how family, grief, and intimacy tangle and transform us. This genre-bending collection expertly utilizes the urgency of playwriting, prose's deep interiority, and poetry's stark surrealness. Its lyrical language will leave you audibly gasping as you fly through its pages. *Burning the Ghost Light* is hands down one of the most honest and inventive collections I've read in years."

— KELLY GRACE THOMAS, author of *Boat Burned*

" 'The heart is a verb that fragments / howls,' writes Caitlin Conlon in this clear-eyed & scintillatingly original sophomore collection. *Burning the Ghost Light* insists upon the integrity of its documentation, interrogating the senseless & earned griefs of its players with extraordinary precision & empathy. Across four acts that increasingly rupture the ever-porous boundary between speaker & subject, a mirror held up to the mother reflects the beloved; forward motion into healing gives way to the lingering blisters of childhood neglect; the performer's shimmering mask drops as the velvet curtain rises. With a gift for plucking improbable tendernesses from the mundane landscapes of memory, Conlon's speakers haunt & hallow the stages they inhabit, in all their fragmentation & howling. This book dives fearlessly into the rippling undertow of the self—& on the brink of drowning, it breaks the surface of the water, re-emerges gasping & alive."

— TOPAZ WINTERS, author of *So, Stranger* and *Portrait of My Body as a Crime I'm Still Committing*

# BURNING THE GHOST LIGHT

POEMS

CAITLIN CONLON

central avenue
2025

This book is a work of creative expression. Although it draws upon the author's personal experiences, it includes fictionalized elements, alterations, and composite characters for literary effect. As such, it should not be read as a literal or factual account. Any resemblance to actual persons, living or dead, or to actual events is purely coincidental or used in a fictionalized manner.

Published by Central Avenue Poetry, an imprint of Central Avenue Marketing Ltd.
centralavenuepublishing.com

**BURNING THE GHOST LIGHT: POEMS**

Trade Paperback: 978-1-77168-416-3
Ebook: 978-1-77168-417-0

Printed in United States of America

1. POETRY / Women    2. POETRY / American

1 3 5 7 9 10 8 6 4 2

*For Ari, my stagehand*

*&*

*For Clara, my acting coach*

*&*

*For Kayla, my set designer*

# CONTENTS

## INTERMISSION



## ACT III - THE LOVER



## ACT IV - THE SELF

## FINAL BOWS

BURNING THE GHOST LIGHT premiered in Buffalo, New York, on September 9th, 2025, at The Round Theatre. The director was Caitlin Conlon. The set design was inspired by a dream the director had, in which she was wandering through an art museum, alone, with no end in sight. Though the set itself does not depict a museum in every scene, it does attempt to replicate that feeling. There was no costume designer for this show; every character was told to choose an outfit from their closet, as long as it was period appropriate. Due to this, the costumes change with every performance. There was no music to accompany this show. The sound design was perfected by a small, delicate bird, seen flying around with ephemera in its beak. The stage managers were chosen not for their managing abilities, but based upon how much they could empathize with the characters. Their names are not important.

## SETTING

Present day. The stage should not try to masquerade as anything other than a stage. Props can be brought in and out as needed, but no major structures are required. The characters should appear vulnerable, without the protection of a background behind them.

To pretend that this is not a performance would be disingenuous to the director's wishes.

## PROP LIST

Shopping cart
Duffel bag, old
Yellow cake with chocolate frosting
Mason jar
How long
Beach towel, striped
Bike helmet with chinstrap
Box full of junk
Archer's bow
Can you
Bouquet of sunflowers
Snow brush
Orange pill bottles
Quilted blanket
Carry
Pair of tap shoes
Umbrella, black
Lanyard with keys
Biology textbook
The past

## DRAMATIS PERSONAE

THE MOTHER

THE MOTHER invents realities where nothing bad has ever happened to her. She often lies awake, long into the night, wondering what she could've been if it wasn't for her body. THE MOTHER was always a mother. Some of us are born that way. THE MOTHER is a character you are rooting for but still become frustrated with. When she interacts with other characters, THE MOTHER should charm them easily. You should walk away from her feeling as though she understands you. Whether or not that's true is beside the point. THE MOTHER speaks as though she is conjuring the words from air in front of her. Your first impression of THE MOTHER should be that you could love her deeply, if only she would let you.

THE FATHER

THE FATHER can breathe underwater. Or, he couldn't but spent his whole life pretending. When he moves, he does so quietly. After THE FATHER became a father, he bought a mirror, six feet tall, and installed it in the new baby's bedroom. Nobody questions THE FATHER'S actions, even when warranted. This is why his story must end the way it does. THE FATHER knows something terrible is going to happen to him, but cannot tell you what. He always looks both ways before crossing the street. Avoids black cats and carries salt in his pocket to throw over his shoulder. Your first impression of THE FATHER should be that he is deeply flawed and occasionally unlikable, but still worthy of empathy.

THE LOVER

THE LOVER must be played by a different actor in every scene, to establish that there are multiple lovers and they are all interchangeable except when they aren't. You'll know when they aren't. THE LOVER should be expressive with their hands when they're speaking to other characters. You should be able to instantly notice their flaws and then promptly ignore them for the rest of the show. THE LOVER should appear largely unperturbed by the events happening on stage. It is imperative that THE LOVER stay in character even when waiting in the wings. Ideally, the audience should fall in love with THE LOVER at least a little bit. Your first impression of THE LOVER should be that, of course, they are wrong for you, but they'll do for now.

THE SELF

THE SELF is a character that could easily fade into the background of the show if not for their reluctant starring role. Though their act is the final one, do not underestimate their impact on every character before them. THE SELF should be seen backstage, silently watching the first three acts of the show. This can be achieved either by setting up a camera which constantly faces them, or by drawing the curtains. THE SELF is the most difficult role to play in the show because they must always be acting, aware that they are performing. The audience should not be privy to how taxing it is to play THE SELF. When they encounter other characters, THE SELF should make themselves smaller in comparison—hunch their shoulders, look downward, etc. Your first impression of THE SELF should be that they are the most relatable person in the room.

DIRECTOR'S NOTE: THE SELF may also be referred to as DAUGHTER, SHE, HER, I, ME, and YOU.

# ACT I
## THE MOTHER

*(Before the act begins, we see THE SELF sitting calmly backstage in a black, folding chair. Their hands rest with palms against knees, their ankles twined together. THE SELF appears poised and perhaps overly careful to the audience, as if THE SELF is afraid of possessing an errant limb or appendage. Afraid that any disruption on their part may halt the show entirely.)*

## IT'S THE SAME OLD STORY ABOUT MOTHERS & DAUGHTERS

THE MOTHER enters from stage left. She changes slowly out of her work attire, slips into a tee shirt, and sits for just a moment too long on the end of her bed, staring ahead all the while

from stage right, her daughter crawls under the same covers and kicks her socks off, bundling them into the sheets like a secret. A voice from the wings asks if she needs anything and the daughter lies

still. Both women are unnervingly quiet, unaware of each other despite their proximity. It's the same old story. Everything we give birth to is capable of killing us.

Consider the word *lightening,* which means both to brighten, and to drop low in the uterus during the final weeks of pregnancy. Consider what it means to be THE MOTHER, sinking,

knowing this is the closest you will ever be to your child before giving them the choice to turn away from you.

THE MOTHER stands and begins to exit stage right, crossing over her daughter in the process. She reaches out a hand, so close to touching her.

But—

## GOOD MEMORIES, OR, THE MOTHER RECEIVES DIRECTOR'S NOTES

When her hands were small enough that she needed
both of them to grip a door handle, you would sprawl
across the mudroom floor and put your shoes on
together. One foot at a time, *shoes on on*, giggling softly
like the brook behind your house.
She knew unequivocally that she was loved.
What a terrible thing to take away.

Your face, so young, glowed with maternal pride.
The fact of her existence was a shining beacon guiding you home,
a place you dared not visit alone in fear of its ghosts
and the secrets they'd ask you to atone for. The mere presence
of her tiny body was divine intervention, saying *Here's proof!*
*You have not ruined everything!*

If the audience looks back with enough focus, they can almost
see your combined shadow tottering across the lawn.
It follows you noiselessly

*[implicit threat]*

until you untangle your limbs.
Right before you push her away
from your chest and separate for good.

## WELCOME TO HANNAFORD, THE GREAT EQUALIZER OF MATERNAL RELATIONSHIPS

Under fluorescent lighting, THE MOTHER ceases to be a source of trauma and becomes just another woman that can't control her children. In this scene, her daughter trails reluctantly behind her, unwilling duckling. THE MOTHER meanders through aisles without urgency, pauses at an end cap, compares boxes of

- ☐ Oatmeal.
- ☐ Strawberry is her favorite but banana is on sale. The daughter only eats oatmeal when she shares breakfast with THE MOTHER, which has dwindled with the loss of her baby fat. They both decide on
- ☐ Banana and share a blessed moment of reprieve from decision-making. Soon they're in the
- ☐ Bread aisle, making small talk about their favorite brands of
- ☐ Peanut Butter. THE MOTHER clings to every minor similarity between herself and her daughter as if they're proof and not coincidence. The daughter, meanwhile, moves on autopilot—it's easier to slog through this tired routine than admit she's already on the car ride home. It's become second nature for her to perform.
- ☐ Cheddar Cheese,
- ☐ Whole Milk, and
- ☐ Yogurt jump into the cart as if to break the tension. In the meat department, the checked-out daughter is startled into the present by her MOTHER's face, reflected next to her own in the cold glass window, which guards the
- ☐ Steak. Through this found mirror she examines THE MOTHER, her head floating between bloody pieces of meat, and notices the series of gray fault lines which thread through her hair. Time is passing by them and into the secure hands of some anonymous higher power. They both wonder, separately and together, *is it too late to change*?

The cart begins to roll away and neither of them notice.

## THE MOTHER & I GO ON A COFFEE DATE

Every barista knows her name. Can make her order exactly how she likes it. They're out of sugar so I use salt instead. It's been months since our last meeting. Long enough to itch my skin raw, waiting for some unknowable "next time." THE MOTHER asks about people I no longer share heartspace with and I lie about how they're doing. Why ruin an afternoon by reminding her that we're strangers? I glance at my watch hoping to find the seconds I've wasted grieving our minor relationship added back onto my clock; not wasted, just deferred. I listen to THE MOTHER's voice, watch her smile widely and take my hand across the table. I love her, which hurts much worse than hating her. There's a brief moment, as her thumb strokes the top of my knuckles, where I almost feel brave enough to say the unspeakable. A brief moment where I am twelve years old again, yearning for a parent to tell me that I am not irreparably broken. But, of course, it passes without incident. I'm too cowardly to admit that I'm drowning. I'd swallow my teeth, chase it with the salt shaker, if it would make everyone else in the room more comfortable.

## MOTHER,

The heart is a verb that fragments
howls
its memories are jagged are splinters in the thumb
poking
the place you left for me to stitch closed
there is a reason the heart is not a metaphor
MOTHER, i haven't heard from
your voice in months this side of your body
mirroring my own

in another lifetime
we could be sisters
swapping secrets and giggling while
time continues descending and our bloodline grows thinner with age

there is too much to bear but it's sunny in our epilogue
MOTHER, you should know
the cold is always colder alone
it's late and i'm rattling the doorknob hoping for an excuse to leave

love is not literature
looking for a page to live on it must be a wound.

## NIGHT TERRORS

Mother's shadow strolls into my bedroom as I stare
patiently at the ceiling waiting for sleep. Her dark
hands sweep over my forehead, and I wish for a good
memory that never comes. I am not afraid
of my mother but there is no avoiding the fact
of her body. How it slides over me, eclipsing
our shared shape.           AH! There it is! Pleasant
recollection! We are reading on the sofa, one mug
on each end table. I gave her a book I adored.
She's reading it because I adored it. Simple joy.
The fictional mother dies and we discuss the grief
with our heads close together. Oh, how I have loved
my mother. With such bite, such bitterness. I close
my eyes to her silhouette, this recalled warmth,
and begin to fade into a dream where
none of this is real.

## MOTHER'S MONOLOGUE

I remember the taste of that afternoon—chocolate
frosting and orange pop in red solo cups, your father
fetching stiff napkins whenever I asked. Even then,
I could feel your vibrant youth and my terrible old age
like a pair of twins festering in my belly. Did you know
I trimmed your fingernails with my teeth for months,
too scared to clip your tiny hands? I accidentally
swallowed, once, and felt your skin
traveling down my throat, scratching my heart raw.
I loved you too much to do it right.

In the kitchen, I bathe myself in the glimmer
of your baby photos, precarious underneath
bulky magnets. This one here is from your first birthday party.
Nobody can tell just by looking but I'm the one with the camera,
the one you're reaching for with inexpressible joy.

If nobody else remembers, I will.

# I VISIT A THRIFT STORE WITH THE MOTHER AND SHE FORGETS HER WALLET

Order 1234
02/22/22

JEANS SIZE 0........................................................$6.95 OR

tell me about the summer
where THE FATHER took you
camping & you ate lobster with bare hands
warm butter making a mess
of you

MIX CD........................................................$2.70 OR

tell me about how they
cleaned the baby before
she met your chest
almost unrecognizable
without blood

CERAMIC COFFEE MUG........................................................$3.47 OR

tell me about the oceans
you crossed
searching for a country
with no word for "daughter"

PICTURE FRAME........................................................$3.75 OR

tell me the difference between
a photograph of my first birthday
party & your memory of it
would you change anything

MASON JAR W/ MISC. ITEMS........................................................$3.10 OR

tell me a lie if it means
I can forgive you

TOTAL........................................................$19.97

## THE MOTHERHOOD PARABLE

Anger is Love's eldest child. Mother
to her siblings. Mother to her Mother.
Anger makes a home of fish bones
gathered from lakes she once tried
to drown herself in. Death is Anger
three times removed. What's left to tell
about families? Love is afraid
of being pulled under the waves but keeps
a jar of seashells on her nightstand.
We want to look our fears in the face
but only if their teeth have been yanked
from their gums. Anger is a terrible liar.
Red-faced and spitting, stricken and cursed.
How do you tell Love they aren't enough?
Anger wants to grow old quietly.
Retire in a house—a real house!—by the sea.
Undisturbed afternoons reading on the beach
to the sound of endless waves. But Anger cannot die
without first making peace with Love.
Eventually you have to look your Mother in the eye
and beg her to let you go. Even if she's gone
already. Even if she trembles at the sight
of you. You and your full, terrible smile,
so much like her own.

## THREE VIGNETTES ON LOSS

I'm on the phone with my mother
            & she's doing this fun thing
where she unburies her trauma
            & asks me if it's breathing.
Because I am the closest iteration she has
            to a parent, I do what any
mother would do.

I let it live. I bury it again.

//

When my grandmother died I gained custody of my mother.
She packed her meager belongings in a duffel bag;
                        the childhood she couldn't bear to release
                        photographs of blurry strangers
                        every one of her baby teeth.
I drove the duffel bag & my mother
to my apartment. I mistakenly cooked a dinner
that she couldn't stomach so I ate it all myself.
My mother cried as she washed our plates,
waving goodbye over and over into the cheap dishrag.

I did what any mother would do.
I remembered.

//

They don't tell you beforehand that motherhood
                        is just learning to grieve
in the least inconvenient way possible.
                        I was my mother's mother
before I was ever her daughter.

## ALMOST SONNET FOR PARALLEL LINES OR MOTHERS & DAUGHTERS

Somebody just has to reach out their————
——We sing the same song in different———
—This relationship traverses rare————
————In my mind we plant magnificent—

———I'm tired of pretending that we are——
————So much time wasted preparing for—
Our evening clothes rumpled, bizarre————
——Between these lines I find your prints, your———

—I'll trade honesty for a perfect————
————I'll dedicate each performance to—
———Audiences forced to reflect——
————I'm stranded within this see-through—

Come find me, please, before I stop————
——That soft noise is the backdrop———

## THE DOG & I HAVE A STARING CONTEST

There's a treat in the darkness but we can't sniff it out.
Now, more than ever, I wish we could communicate.

I'd ask, "When she lets you out of the back door,
does she wait for you to come back? At mealtimes,

does she eat before, after, or with you? Does she tell you
that you're good? How often, and why?"

I used to carry tenderness around like a mangled toy.
Took it in my mouth and dropped it at the feet of anyone

that smelled like home. Forgiveness, too, was a plaything
I once called a gift. Now, I see it is a promise

I must keep practicing the commands for. Work, foremost.
Not a given. I don't forgive you, yet, but I want to.

I will get on my knees and test the theory again.

## THE MOTHER RECEIVES AN INVITATION

We don't have to talk about it—the missed dance recitals
and band concerts, how we cried so terribly that one summer
while stalling in the driveway, sunlight striking our shoulders
as if to punish us. Let's take a walk before dinner,
around the lake behind your old house. Remember
when that swan chased us through the exit? How we'd chant
*lions and tigers and bears, oh my!* next to wooded areas of the trail,
casting a spell to keep us safe? Well, no matter. There's no need
to pick us apart any more than I already have. Here,

I've made us a meal.
There's warm bread and olive oil, speckled with spices, perfect for dipping.
Forgiveness will be joining us, so hurry up and get dressed.
Please don't worry about a thing.

I'm missing you already.

*SET CHANGE*

*(THE MOTHER and THE FATHER stand in front of a painting while the set change happens behind them. Neither of them notice the stagehands—it's as if nobody else exists. THE MOTHER and THE FATHER have not seen each other in 22 years, but neither of them acknowledges this fact. The content of the painting itself is irrelevant. They look together.)*

THE MOTHER. Do you think we did the best we could, given the circumstances?

*(A beat.)*

THE FATHER. I don't think there's an easy way to answer that.

*(THE MOTHER steps closer to the painting. Does not face the audience.)*

THE MOTHER. You know, it's not my fault for leaving. You never gave me a choice.

THE FATHER. It was never your fault for *leaving*. It was your fault for coming back.

*(THE MOTHER is surprised by this answer. She considers its implications before responding, hurt.)*

THE MOTHER. That's funny, coming from someone who isn't going to live until the end of the show.

*(THE FATHER turns away from the painting, and we see his face for the first time.)*

THE FATHER. Don't spoil it.

*(End of scene.)*

# ACT II
## THE FATHER

*(For the entirety of this act THE SELF is seen backstage, in the same folding chair from the previous act, drinking a large glass of water. The water is so cold that the glass appears wet and difficult to grip. During the final scene of this act, THE SELF will finish the glass of water, rise to their feet, place the empty glass on the seat of the folding chair, then exit the stage entirely.)*

## IN THE DEEP END

THE FATHER teaches me how to swim, his arms an orchard drowning
in rain. I dive into the pool, suck in the silence, unravel my nerves.

THE FATHER tells me to point my toes. I point my toes. He watches.

THE FATHER was a good father up close. Once you panned out, once
you toweled off and sat in the sun for an hour, he became a man

capable—as they all are—of leaving. His vibrant, nylon pockets never

held slabs of stone but he did carry bags of pebbles. Even now,
I take them into the deep end and try to fight my inheritance.

If only I kick a little harder, hold my breath a little longer, point my

blue toes a little straighter, then I'll be able to rewrite the ending.
Not facedown in a cool drink. No, I will hold the killing thing.

I will swallow it.

THE FATHER, when I was no older than duckling, would pick me
up, squirming and giggling, and toss me into the deep end.

Every time I surfaced, I never had to doubt that he'd be there,

waiting. What I'm trying to say is that if dying were a choice
he would not have taken it.

## WHAT THE FATHER TAUGHT ME

When you open a green pepper, slice a sharp knife along the white edges.
Its seeds won't kill you, but you still don't want to eat them.

If you're scraping ice from your windshield, you should also scrape your
headlights.

Most daughters are born from heartache. Not all, but most.

Details matter.

Drive with the flow of traffic.

Tell them you love them but only if you love them.
(Did you love them? Did you tell them?)

Pedal harder if the bike begins to wobble. Wear a helmet, fasten
the chinstrap.

Life is just a cluster of bell pepper seeds in a cupped palm.

When the baseball curves in your direction, keep your feet planted.

A memory without context is a dangerous ghost.

It's okay to be a little sentimental. Save the notes, trinkets.

If your future begins to look like your father's, your natural reaction will be
to bow your head and accept it.

Avoid the heart of your pain if you want to survive.

If you want to survive, you inherited that from me.

## THE FATHER IS OUTLIVED BY HIS FAVORITE TV SHOW

Alex, I'll take **GRIEF IN THE SHOWER** for 400.

*(I'll take myself back to thinking THE FATHER was*
*indestructible, and then I'll take myself back to*
*thinking he was irredeemable, and then I'll take myself*
*home, which is somewhere in-between.)*

THIS MONTH IS THE LAST TIME YOU HUGGED THE FATHER, ALSO KNOWN FOR STICKY WEATHER AND CELEBRATING ALLEGED AMERICAN FREEDOM.

What is July?

Alex, I'll take **STARING AT THE TEXT THREAD** for 1200.

*(I'll take a shot of vodka and another*
*shot of vodka and pretend there isn't*
*a part of my body that could keep going and keep going and*
*keep going and keep going and)*

THE NUMBER OF TIMES YOU USED THE WORD "LOVE" IN THE LAST YEAR OF YOUR FATHER'S LIFE.

What is ten and a half?

Alex, I'll take **THE AFTERMATH** for 2000.

*(I'll take it all, Alex.*
*I need some answers.*
*I really need some answers.)*

THIS QUESTION HAS PLAGUED THE BEREAVED ACROSS TIME, ACROSS OCEANS, ACROSS LANGUAGE.

What happens to my name when the person who chose it succumbs to a deathblow?

Alex, what if the deathblow sounds like ice clinking in a glass?

What if the answer I've been searching for is just another question?

## THE FATHER SHOWS HIS HAND

Because I'm two years away from a driver's license,
every Friday night at 8 PM, THE FATHER has to drive me home
from his apartment. Home to my grandmother who waits

with the television on, gray sweatpants cinched around her soft
waist, expecting. Because I'm two years away from
a driver's license and don't realize that I'm allowed to make

a scene, I get into the passenger seat of his bright green car
even though I know THE FATHER has had three glasses already,
mixed expertly with trembling hands

while I sat on the couch with a laptop warming my thighs.
THE FATHER is angry because I've asked him to buy a case of oranges
to help fundraise for my band trip to Chattanooga. He thinks

my grandmother is trying to steal his money, forgetting that
she holds onto silence when he neglects the child
support check. At the bottom of a glass, all THE FATHER

can see is his own reflection, scratchy from the violence
of a life spent reaching. I grip the handle of the door as he
drives, focusing on the street signs. There are only three red

lights between THE FATHER's apartment and the house I grew
up in. He mumbles to himself as if I'm not even there and maybe
I'm not. THE FATHER runs a red light on Baseline while cars honk

around us. I want to be pulled over so the buildings will stop
blurring but don't want to be pulled over because when THE
FATHER yells I become a ghost. But, of course, there is no

stopping anger in motion. THE FATHER has driven under the
influence enough times to get from point a to point b without hassle.
Ten years after leaving his apartment we pull into

the driveway of my childhood home. The windows are lit
and twinkling, as if a lighthouse was dropped in the middle
of a field. THE FATHER and I open and shut our respective

doors without discussion, unzipping noise from the quiet
night. The clicks are like ice cubes, clinking against
the shrinking glass of my adolescence.

## SOMEWHERE IN THE OUTERSPHERE

My father's energy is solidifying.
He has a torso, and two eyes. With time he'll have hands and
maybe a throat.

Somewhere in the innersphere I'm grieving the future. My pens
lose ink faster than I can replace them. I never wanted tradition,
but I cry on Kenwood Ave when I realize I'll never share a walk
down an aisle with my father. The final item on his bucket list,
uncrossed forever.

Somewhere in the outersphere my father does not remember that he
is a father. He's gripping stars until they beg for space. Gravity
tugs at his body and he submits to its whims as it pulls him down,
only down.

Somewhere in the innersphere I'm tearing apart my split ends
with a bereaved vengeance. Someone in my family took the map
of Ireland off my father's wall and nobody knows where it ended
up. I crossed an ocean to give it to him and nobody knows where
it ended up. I crossed an ocean. Nobody knows. It ended.

(In the most outer of outerspheres I scream obscenities at everyone
who denied me closure.)

Somewhere in the innersphere I acknowledge that sometimes
you have to choose yourself. My father knew this. Chose
himself even when he didn't want to, and I suppose there were times where
he didn't want to. Choosing yourself can be an act
of violence. Why else call it a choice?

## CLUTTERED INTIMACY

I steal trinkets from the makeshift Goodwill donation
box when my family isn't looking. Stash the petty
trash of my late father's belongings in coat
pockets and pretend to unhand the past.

I steal items without memories
so their proximity won't make me cry.
But he still touched them. Still kept them.

I am not a thief but I am sentimental and
maybe that's the same thing. The kitchen table,
buckling under the weight of a life
cut short, has a scratch running down its center.

My father never seated himself at the head
of his own dining room. The signs were all there.
I should've known our history would kill us eventually.

In the glove box of my car, I shove a lovingly engraved
flask, hungry maw gasping for air, into its depths.
Its unique history is a knowledge I will never obtain.

This, too, is a type of clutter.

## A QUICK NOTE ON THE FATHER'S PERFORMANCE

Now that I can't look the beast in the eye or smell the booze on its breath, I keep slipping into sentimentality. Nostalgia builds a comfortable bed and I pull the covers over my eyes with glee. Please don't make me remember the ceiling cracks or the shouting. The way he arrived drunk at my grandmother's funeral after disappearing for months. A warm corpse in the ground, and he was parenting a bottle of vodka. If I talk about that, I have to acknowledge the phone calls where no personal questions were asked of me. We made small talk and sat, hushed, for years, until I found an excuse to hang up. How do you make normal conversation with the man that could not sober up enough to drive your young body home safely? Images of him stumbling down the stairs and hugging teddy bears reeking of cigarette smoke weasel into even the best memories. I can't do it. Don't make me look in the mirror yet. Let me write THE FATHER as if he was just a decent person capable of mistakes and not a painful root twined around my ankles. I loved him, yes, I loved him, but not without tears. He made me cry, once, after I called my stepfather "Dad." *That man is not your Dad*, he said, roughly.

What about now?

# MY FATHER DIED & I INHERITED ALL OF HIS SINUS ISSUES

My father, easily sunburned, boozy, un-
known, passes into aftermath between white
sheets, alone in a room while, miles away,

I fidget on a pull-out bed. Months later,
his body ash, I feel the temperature change
before the thermometer does. Weather drains

down the back of my throat, obstructs
my breathing until I'm forced to spit clouds
into the sink, blow thunderstorms

into tissues. I study my reflection
and see my father's nose, his bad eyesight,
his stubbornness. As a child, I loved him

more than I would ever love him again.
As a child I wanted nothing more
than to be like the people I came from,

not knowing what I'd be forced to carry.
Now, my wish is granted. I can predict cold
spells by the timbre of my swallow. I can feel

the whole world clogging up my cavities, taking
over my body. And I hate it. I hate telling stories.
I hate knowing what's coming, and not being able

to change a thing.

# ARCHERY LESSON HAIBUN

They put a bullseye on his liver. Took scans and filed paperwork and provided a chart with arrows that emerged in retrograde. They called it cirrhosis but I knew that was just another word for love. THE FATHER, the alcoholic, does not tell me about the bullseye, or the liquor, or how the doctors gave him a range of time with a definite ending. What he does talk about are the tomatoes he planted in the community garden, their trellises like blooming crucifixes. THE FATHER is a religious man and by that I mean he believes in forgiveness. And by that I mean when I get the call to come now, get in the car, he forgives me for hesitating. He forgives me for not knowing what to do, other than read Stephen King at his bedside. He forgives me for filing the moment away for a poem that has become this one. I could not love THE FATHER without reservation until we were alone in the hospice room—his body almost motionless, his hands without watering can. As blue jays chattered outside the window I quietly, kindly, drew the bow and arrow to my chest.

Aiming for his heart
I opened my pitted hands.
I let it all go.

## PORTRAIT OF MY FATHER AS A YOUNG MAN

I don't know any of this for certain. But
it's possible that my father, a young man,
eager to stretch into futures bigger than
a bottle, tangled his fingers in a seine net
and lifted it on a count of three. I lied,
I do know a few things for certain. My father
worked on a shrimp boat in his early twenties.
Stayed at a friend's apartment in Biloxi.
He told me that when Katrina blew through
he watched that same apartment drown
from the comfort of his New York living room
broadcast on the Weather Channel.
Okay, back to what I don't know. Maybe
the boat had a name. Something dreamy.
My father could've watched seagulls
following his wake every morning.
Thought them something other than nuisance,
or just nuisance, or just thought of them
in a way that only he could. Perhaps he wore
a raincoat the color of red wine. Perhaps
he grew to love the salt that stuck to his skin,
like dew on a cold glass. When my father
talked about the past it was as if he molded it
himself, knuckles deep in creation. I could
never tell how he actually felt about anything.
It's entirely possible that during his years
on the water he held a live shrimp in his raw,
red hands. And maybe as he was doing this,
the sun reflected brilliantly upon the sea,
a mirror, and he saw himself. And for a
moment, he could've been happy.

He could've been so happy.

# ON BEING ASKED ABOUT YOUR FATHER BY SOMEBODY THAT DOES NOT KNOW HE IS DEAD

My father's face emerges from
an emerald lake, laden with
seaweed and smelling of fish.

He takes a hesitant breath
and I, trembling,
reach out a hand
and push him back down
again.

# GENESIS

In the beginning, my father treaded the water of his life with chin held high.
Then his voice drained, became shallow enough
to stand up in. Eventually he had to sit down.

Death is a careless thief.
It takes everything except what's killing you.

The last time I saw my father conscious
he looked at me like I was a ghost
haunting his bedside. Even then, half-gone,
we still had the same nose. As if to divide
my blood from his I repeated my name
on a loop, hoping it would register
in the part of his body that still
remembered creating me.

Our parents create us, then we create our
parents. It wasn't until my father forgot my
silhouette that I was able to complete
his features. Months later, peering into the blue lake
where I drowned his ashes

I could finally see who he was.

## FATHER'S MONOLOGUE*

I have never b e e
n indestructible,
so
I replace d
a hand
But could
not sober . As if to divide
my presence
from Yo u r love

*THE FATHER'S monologue is composed of phrases and letters from existing poems. We cannot know what THE FATHER would say if given a stage. He is gone.

# INTERMISSION

*(There are no set movements or actions that THE SELF must complete during intermission. They may stretch, complete breathing exercises, or go over notes with the director, though none of this is required. Regardless of whether THE SELF is in frame or not, the audience must have viewing access of their black, folding chair.)*

## THE AUDIENCE READS THEIR PROGRAMS WHILE THE LOVER PACES THE STAGE, ANXIOUS TO BEGIN

Imagine, Ophelia never climbs the tree.
Grief-stricken, heavy with loss, she deadens
the noise of her screams among red clover
and shrubbery. In the safe wilderness
of the forest that bordered her earliest years,
she practices bloodletting. She tells Hamlet
to get his head out of his ass. As men argue
like children in the castles of her youth,
Ophelia gathers her dress and walks past
the branch that could become her folly,
the choice that could become her legacy.
It was never written, but Ophelia loved
to swim. She'd steal away under night's
cloak and strip down to her skin, allow
the water of the brook to caress her weary
shoulders and the soft skin between her breasts.
Imagine, Ophelia does not become a metaphor
for the mad woman. She is never found. Instead,
she carries herself down to the bank. Leaves
her adolescence in the dirt. Imagine, Ophelia
takes a running leap, holds her breath, then cuts
into the water's surface like an arrow.
Under the blue, where nobody can see her,
she smiles.

# ACT III
## THE LOVER

*(THE SELF appears stiff and uncomfortable, standing and sitting and pacing about, for the duration of this act, even during scenes which depict moments of joy. After the final scene, the stage will go dark and a spotlight will fully illuminate THE SELF for the first time. The audience acknowledges that THE SELF is crying, though not uncontrollably. The spotlight will accompany THE SELF for the remainder of the show.)*

## I WAS SEVENTEEN

I was seventeen and sat in front of THE LOVER in English class. In English class I learned that THE LOVER's favorite poet was Allen Ginsberg. Allen Ginsberg wrote a poem about a sunflower, which THE LOVER recited to the class, one week after my presentation on William Blake, who also wrote a poem about a sunflower. *Sunflower O my soul, I loved you then!* is what THE LOVER recited to the class, and I knew I was in trouble. Trouble, because the rest is history. History is what I live in when the present is too unpredictable. Unpredictable and with a stupid green thumb pressed against my stupid budding heart, THE LOVER and I sidestepped around the future. The future is what I live in when the present is too predictable. Predictable, as always, I loved a boy without knowing his body. His body that I studied with a gardener's eye, frothing at the mouth as he handled his Toyota Camry's stick shift. Shift to years later and I'm catching up with an old friend. An old friend, who is one of the only people I keep in touch with from when I was seventeen. I was seventeen, she says, when he hurt me, and I don't ask who. But she tells me anyway. Anyway, remember him? Him? Him. Him, I repeat. Repeat it. It echoes. Echoes like a story born in the back of my throat. My throat, that I presented as a gift, wanting to be held. Held like I am by these memories that grip me like a vase, taste in the mouth of burnt soil and shame. Shame because I know with certainty that I'm capable of loving terrible people. Terrible people can love good poems and hide behind bouquets. Bouquets of fake smiles, plastic leaves, all wrong. All wrong in my head because I don't automatically think of the ending, but the beautiful beginning. The beautiful beginning, when my fingers were petals and I was only seventeen. I was only seventeen and sat in front of THE LOVER and it could have been me. It could have been me crying on his porch and it wasn't me. It wasn't me and I hate myself for feeling relieved. Relieved that it wasn't me. It wasn't me and I loved him and I didn't know. I didn't know and then I did. I did, and then I couldn't. I couldn't, and I can't.

## "WOULD IT HAVE KILLED YOU TO CALL ME PRETTY INSTEAD?"

You told me that someone would find me beautiful someday.
Careful words, so careful I didn't know what you really meant
until years later. What if we'd stripped ourselves clean
on your couch instead of just thinking about it? Would I feel less shame
about my body, or more? LOVER, I remember everything.
I remember how it felt to be the one you held
when you were sad but not the one underneath your exhale.
I remember needing to be kissed so badly I would cry
imagining the possibility. I didn't think it would ever happen
for me, LOVER—my face cradled and breakable. But now,
someone is in love with me. They call me
pretty and I can't help but think they're lying. What do they see
that you couldn't? Last night, I dreamt us in the past. My loose hair
on your pillowcase, a series of ghostly commas. Your smoke
dancing with the ceiling fan. We almost kissed.

Didn't.

# WHAT IT WAS LIKE

He asked to borrow my snow brush.
Doe-eyed and sheepish, snow collecting in his beard,
in that moment I'd have given anything he asked of me—
thankfully, it was only a hand.

No immediate spark lit between us, no brief yet
brilliant exchange of energy, though I tried
to write it into our script later on.
He cleared the snow from his windshield with
short movements, like the minute hand of a broken
clock twitching anxiously in place.
I wish I'd kissed him then, before it could hurt me.

Weeks later, we ate greasy pizza in the glow
of his television, licking our fingers and giggling as if
our futures weren't some shade of dead. I let him slide
the scrunchie from my hair, unfurl curls over the navy blue
of his bedsheets. I have slept on the left side of every bed
since. I was damned before ever counting my ribs
in his bathroom mirror, damned from the second
I watched his newly clean car drive smoothly into
the dark.

Sometimes, still, the moon falls onto my face
and it reminds me of what it was like to want him.
He's the urgency in every emergency,
spiraling gleefully past my front door.

## FRIENDS ON VENMO

We haven't spoken in eight years but I know you paid
your internet bill last month. I know your girlfriend—
who shares my name but spells it wrong—
reimbursed you for margaritas on Cinco de Mayo.
She uses emojis I didn't know existed. I can't speak your language
anymore, can't imagine you outside of your transaction history.
You gave me midnight fantasies and I gave you a story to tell
at parties. *She loved me*, you might say. Or, juicier,
*I was her first love*, which I never spoke but can confirm now
is true. Years of my life spent nursing our conversations.
Finding you in every high school hallway and I still dream us new
meetings. Our backs pressed to evergreen lockers and lips twined
like teenagers. I show friends you'll never meet the message
you wrote in my yearbook. Omit how I cried for my name
in your cursive hand. We have no mutual transactions. Why
did we become friends in the first place? I send $150
to Kayla for our hotel room in Chicago. I send rent to my partner.
I think of you in the Uber ride home and tip the driver through PayPal.
I keep every payment public. I give, and receive,
and give again.

## YES, PAST LOVERS, I STILL DREAM ABOUT YOU

Your hands on the stick shift
Your apartment thick with smoke
Your arms around my waist when I could still stand to be touched
You parade through my unconscious with little fanfare—
as if being there, with me, is normal
I kiss those of you I never got to
Say the things I wrote into poems hoping you'd find it on accident
Do you look for me on bookstore shelves?
Did you keep the things I made you?
LOVERS,
I feel so lonely sometimes
I can't help but look at the past in shades of oleander
Beautiful, yes
But you almost killed me, each in your own way
The memory of your laugh
Mouth
Body
An earworm unshakable
I wake with tears, even now

I see your ghost and raise you immortality

## LOVER'S FERMENTATION

At Junior's Bar & Grill I flirt with my father's
murderer, not for the first or last time.

The aftertaste of a killer is intoxicating—
less than half an hour in the dark & I'm his

until I come up with a reason to stop asking for more.
I run my thumb gently along his lip & bring it

to my own as strangers sidestep around us.
Despite how it may look to the bartender

I'm taking it slow, swirling the evening around,
breathing in its body. By midnight I abandon my family

history. I slide my tongue down his homicidal neck,
bringing every drop of him into me

like I'm on the brink of dehydration, lost in the desert
of my own tipsy grief. Cold hand over wet mouth,

we sway to the jukebox that accepts credit cards but no cash.
We oxidize, grow stale, keep up the charade until it's finally over.

Like a headache, his presence kneads at my skin, changing
my chemistry even as I pull away. & when I do, I'm still left

with the residual sugar of our affair, settled on the bottom
of a glass that I push between my palms. I attempt to read

its pattern as though it can predict the future. Death by
choking? Death by genetics?

How will I know when it's over?

## THIS MIGHT BE THE LAST ONE

Empty orange bottles roll around in the backseat, rattling with every pothole. I'm driving to meet THE LOVER at Tim Hortons. It's been six months of chameleoning myself into the background of my life. I never killed myself, though I thought about it. No more therapist, but I write THE LOVER'S name on every Zoloft so I feel obligated to swallow. Zero trace of THE LOVER except for what I carry on my back. Can't remember what THE LOVER wore to this, our final meeting, but can still taste the lemonade I sipped. How we stood and contemplated the plastic menu boards together—such mundane bullshit. Yes, I loved too hard and too fast. Grieved four times the length of the relationship just to wake up one day and ask for closure. It was kind of THE LOVER to give it to me after all the miserable texts, all the poems where I tried to make him a villain instead of a boy, younger than I am as I rewrite this. At the end, we left in different cars. I vowed never to go back, then returned forty-five minutes later because I'd left my purse at the table we'd haunted. No waiting ghosts, just my wallet and my ID. A discarded straw wrapper and a water-stained ring too big for a finger. I keep writing about this because it's all I have. I loved THE LOVER and now I don't. What am I supposed to do with the memories I baptized, thinking, one day, they'd be holy?

## LOVER'S MONOLOGUE

We've romanticized each other so much it's hard to remember what actually happened, what I actually whispered to you as we sat comatose in your car. Time has only complicated matters, splitting the past into smaller and smaller pieces with each memory we try to call into the present. Love makes unwilling inventors out of everyone it touches.

Do you remember that sign we passed, off the highway somewhere near Syracuse, that read "LAST CHANCE"? It was an omen too perfect to be ignored but we were so caught up in each other back then. Late nights and early mornings. Breakfasts in bed and sunsets sinking into rivers. I woke up every day and felt like I was dying.

In a poem, you asked the page where I was now. Here's your answer.
Sometimes I live in your dresser, among your tee shirts and jeans.
Sometimes I live in a country you've never heard of.
Sometimes I live in the place where you left me to rot. Sometimes—

I can't do this, I'm sorry. None of that is real. None of that happened. I can't conjure metaphors and dreams and pretend they actually happened to us. I'm . . . *[mouths offstage]* line? *[stares intently, then nods]*

. . . not you.

## AT THE KARAOKE BAR

There's a daydream I used to have, where we're in the same bar and I'm actually able to sing. I stand onstage and can't see you in the crowd—but you see me. *She's more beautiful than I remember,* you think, and you're flooded with a movie reel, featuring the first time we pressed against each other in a theater. How I put my foot in my mouth afterward, revealed my hand was full of jokers, and you kissed me anyway. In the fantasy, I picked a song that was obviously about our relationship. The notes rip out of me and you regret leaving. I never imagined further than that. It's about the performance of redemption more than the actuality.

Now, I go to karaoke with my friends and belt words that don't remind me of you. Or, they do, but that's not why I'm singing them. I dance too much, so out of breath I can barely say the lyrics, let alone arrange the notes correctly. I climb on the table, avoiding our drinks, and hope beyond hope that the memory of my body, shrinking in the driver's seat as you slammed the door behind you, gives you hell.

This life without you is better than anything I could have written.

## DELETED SCENES FROM THE LOVER'S ACT

**SCENE II: "Grieftangled."** THE LOVER wakes with bedsheets twisted around limbs. Body a knot tied tight. They turn on their side, careful not to jostle the mattress, and face the only window, situated above a second body sleeping next to them. Artificial light pours in, casting a glow on their face. Nothing to catch it with but their hands. Their pitiful hands.

**SCENE VI: "Spoonspent."** She goes to the diner where she and THE LOVER spent their first date and stays until closing, stirring a cup of decaf until the symphony dissolves. The waitress gives her a new spoon, dull with use, alongside each refill. She wonders what it would be like to take the waitress's apron off in the storage room one string at a time. Press her flush against the refrigerator, so cold. So cold. When she hands over the check, their fingers touch.

**SCENE X: "Fatestruck."** Years after the final splitting, she gets in the car and drives without a destination. She passes towns with names she can't pronounce. Pulls over in a gas station parking lot to cry. We see her face change as a thought careens into her head. At the same time, on the opposite side of the stage, a spotlight illuminates THE LOVER, who is suddenly frozen in the act of preparing dinner. We are meant to understand that, somehow, both of these characters are realizing the same thing simultaneously. They open their mouths to speak in unison, but neither of them have microphones. What they realize is too quiet for any audience to hear.

## MORNING ROUTINE

When I rise from bed, the cat leaping off the edge behind me, I make
quick work of removing all evidence that I was there.
While you sleep, I smooth out layers of blankets and sheets
that I stole under cover of darkness, before arranging them carefully
around your body. Every morning I become the florist to your
garden. I slip into my clothes, not daring to breathe or go flat
on my feet or even glance in your direction. I am so afraid
of the animal love makes of us. How it sleeps so gently.

I know I am more fire than earth. I know that I cause problems
just to prove you can solve them. In the silence of dawn's glow,
I can desire you in peace. Admit to the rise and fall of your chest
that there's nowhere I'd rather be. Intimacy lingers on my tongue
like a mouthful of sunflowers, too bitter to chew.

Across the room, unmoving, it often feels like this is the closest
I will ever get to you. Closer, even, than when you twist your
vines around my waist and tug me to the center of you,
which is also the center of me. Our shared company
is a nocturnal plant that you water when I can't bear to look at it.
I make my way over to your calm and untie the string
around your stems. As if it does not pain me
to know you're real after all.

## THE LOVER'S FINALE, VERSION 1–999,999

THE LOVER & I meet somewhere far in the future.
We choose a museum, crowded with dinosaur bones
and artifacts of human echoes. It's easier to admit
we weren't meant to last when surrounded by endings.
We picnic in the cafeteria. Over wilted salads
and bottled pop, the reminiscing commences.
There were bad times, yes, but there were good
times too. I loved you terribly and you were cruel
and somehow we survived.
Some loves just shouldn't exist in the future.
But we'll always have this—standing in the center
of the universe with tears on our faces,
looking intently at the same remarkable memory.

## THE LOVER'S FINALE, VERSION ONE IN A MILLION

I want to be young with you. A pair of high schoolers
driving around our small town because there's nothing
better to do, or kids in a park making mud pies. Take me
to a place where I can love you without maturity. A place
where we don't have to worry about money and can get married
on a playground with a tree officiating. Lover, I wish
I'd known you my whole life. We could've been twenty-five and stupid
together, nineteen and even stupider. I want all of the years back,
all of them, and I want to know you here, and here, and here, too.
I'm tired of growing at different rates—give me adolescent
mistakes and twenty-two-year-old fights. Take me back so I can
figure out how we got here, you and me, my sweet thing,
my understudy turned lead. It is so hard to be yours sometimes,
it makes me want to strip down to my bones and scream
until the floorboards split. But I keep choosing this life over
and over again. This terrible and beautiful life, with these
unbearable adulthoods blossoming in close proximity.
Your knee against mine as I finish the poem.

## SET CHANGE

*(THE LOVER and THE SELF are standing in front of the painting that THE MOTHER and THE FATHER were studying earlier. This time, there is no activity happening around them. The stage is silent, as if they were standing in a field of snow.)*

*(THE LOVER moves as if to speak, but stops before doing so.)*

THE SELF. What?

THE LOVER. I—never mind.

*(A beat.)*

THE SELF. *(quietly)* I hate when you do that.

THE LOVER. Do what?

THE SELF. Stop yourself in the middle of a thought. Why can't you ever just say what you mean?

THE LOVER. Say what I mean? This whole thing *(gestures wildly around them)* is a metaphor and you want me to just say what I mean?

THE SELF. You don't think a metaphor can tell the truth?

THE LOVER. Not completely.

THE SELF. What if I said that after our first kiss I became a bird, collecting shiny ephemera from the landmarks of my past, and made a nest from the best parts?

THE LOVER. I'd say that was impossible.

*(A beat.)*

THE SELF. We will never understand each other.

# ACT IV
## THE SELF

*(THE SELF departs the stage after the set change, as if their act is not the only one remaining. Before taking the stage again, THE SELF is given a hand mirror—the audience cannot see who delivers it to them. THE SELF cycles through a range of emotions, as if practicing, before placing the mirror facedown on the folding chair. THE SELF swallows, hard.)*

## INTRODUCING: THE ILLUSIVE SELF

THE SELF enters stage left.
THE SELF exits stage right.
THE SELF enters stage right.
THE SELF exits stage left.
THE SELF enters stage left.
THE SELF considers exiting.
THE SELF looks for something to hide behind.
Moves the air that's ziplocked around her body,
combing through its wreckage.
THE SELF goes to climb off the stage,
finds bold, yellow police tape blocking the way.
There is nowhere to go.
THE SELF reluctantly takes center stage or, rather, it takes her.
The spotlight is bright and she visibly sweats.
Everyone is eager for her long-awaited performance.
The invisible hero of the show—her fingertips on every character before.

What will THE SELF say when there are no metaphors or props to hide behind?

# ENTER, STAGE LEFT

Here I am, again,
bewildered by memory,
how it migrates from
my brain, to my body,
and then the unknown.
Ask me how I am
and I will tell you—fine.
Ask me where I came from
and I will kneel at the altar
of my unpredictable grief.
I can't say why I act
this way; I don't know and
I'm too scared to go digging.
I might unearth something
I'm glad I've forgotten.

## THE SELF RETURNS HOME

None of the people that raised me
still live in my hometown except
for my grandmother, buried in its
dirt. When I visit, mostly to prove
that I remember what was done to me,
I sleep between walls that never saw my
thumb-sucking days, over carpets
too rough for bare feet. Even here,

where it began, the world continues
to chew and spit up my past, delivering it
wet and mangled next to my morning
coffee. I can't help but think that I don't
belong anywhere. That if I wake up one day
and decide I don't want this life after all,
I won't have anywhere familiar
to run to. No set of coordinates with

welcoming arms, or buildings without
smell. What do you call a place
where not one person in its vicinity
has wiped tears from your red face,
but you still know when to swerve
and avoid its potholes? What does it mean
that I bring flowers to the graveyard
and there isn't anywhere to put them down?

## THERE'S THIS STORY SHE TELLS

I can't have been older than seven. No dance class in the summer but
I carried my tap shoes everywhere.
Tap, tap, tap on the kitchen floor.
Tap, tap, tap, on the concrete front porch.

I told my grandmother and her neighbor to
sit and watch my recital routine. All's well
until a quick step out
of place,
an eight count
unremembered.
Tears. Curtain drawn and shoes tucked away
two minutes earlier than scheduled.

When she tells the story it is a comedy—
*Can you believe it?*
*How she needed everything to be perfect.*
She's holding the cue cards:
**Laughter! Laughter!**

Dusty size smalls grow stale in a bag rank with shame.
Living room stage permanently dark,
and my child face buried in my arms.

I don't think I'm in the right genre.

I don't know where I belong.

## THE MUNDANE

The grocery store is proof that I am taking care of myself, or, my presence in the grocery store is proof. The building is just a god. In the grocery store I run my teeth along the edge of possibility, compare the benefits of brie to gouda as if they don't both equate to an hour of minimum wage work. In the grocery store, I look like someone that has their shit together. Not a depressed person crying to a song that's heavy-handed with the piano—I have strawberries in my cart. Do depressed people eat strawberries? I pick out the three cartons with the reddest berries, as if to further prove that I'm an adult. Nobody here knows that I rarely went grocery shopping as a child. They don't know that mental illness has devastated my memory so much that I have to walk each aisle twice to remember everything on the list. The umbrella hanging from my arm swings out, hitting the shelves, a melody of competence. I want to say, Look at me! Do I seem sad to you? Do I wear my grief like a trench coat, every past version of myself stacked on my shoulders? No! I have strawberries and yogurt in my cart. I am contemplating pasta sauce. I am pretending because that is my survival tactic: if you can fake it in the grocery store, you can trust yourself to drive straight home. You can trust yourself to eat the food before it rots, so you can go back to the grocery store and act some more. Here's the truth: I hang mirrors in every room of my home—even the kitchen. If nobody is watching me, I can't trust myself to stay alive.

# SPOTLIGHT

THE SELF still has the key to their childhood house
swinging on the end of their lanyard, slicing
the present into jagged pieces.

THE SELF isn't consciously regressive, just
thoughtless. Too enmeshed with the past to notice
the deep scratches down their arms. Years after

THE SELF begins calling a new address home,
they stick the wrong key—their first key—into
the apartment door. They almost break its metal teeth
before realizing their mistake.

Grief is not strong enough to open a lock, but
it can still bring you to your knees. THE SELF,
a pretender even when the curtain's closed, bows
grandly at the waist. THE SELF dips just low enough
that the slight quiver of their bottom lip is rendered
invisible.

## THE SELF ATTEMPTS AN UNSCRIPTED MONOLOGUE

I've never asked for anything real—only the happy dream,

the distant future miraging against the backdrop of my bedroom.

Believe me when I say I'd rather live in a fantasy than sleep soundly

beside my decisions. If I must reside in this dwelling—this life—

then I will erect every reverie I desire. You cannot evict me

from a house that I built. Those are my tears dripping

from the leaky kitchen faucet. My spine in the garden,

trellis for your poison ivy.

## SELF'S MONOLOGUE (SCRIPTED)

When childhood was still perpetual summer and not a darkness
festering, nothing was a metaphor except for my parents—characters

in a story, unfinished caricatures of tired tropes. Nothing was a metaphor
because none of my experiences were like anything else.

There is an unmistakable instant where you pass into adulthood.
This sensation is different for everyone and impossible to prevent.

In dreams, both of my parents are still alive. Last night my father took me
to the top of a Ferris wheel and then jumped off it without me. I passed into

adulthood like finding a key for a long-locked room. Turning the knob
only to find that it was empty all along. Inside, I learned the terrible, open

secret, that adulthood is even more perpetual than childhood.
Worse, there's nothing soft to hide behind. You must do it all

yourself.

## CHEKHOV'S GUN

Time has passed even when I've lain on the ground and refused to do anything.

I call offstage for my next line

but there is no curtain, no stagehand with cues. I must remember all by myself and this is what comes to mind: my last morning in South Carolina. I pull over to the side of the road after discovering an empty beach. Out I clamber, shedding shoes and socks as I run into the ocean. I pass through gentle waves—forty feet from shore but still only waist-deep. My frolic is cast in hues of pink and golden shine, dawn unzipping the sky. I had this idea, that I could walk forever into the deep end and my feet would never leave the ground. This was a place where I could finally be alone and, still, part of the world. A willing participant in savoring the moment.

*[My next line comes to me with a violence akin to seasickness. I sit up, and breathe until the words breach.]*

Happiness has always been possible.

## 26

I miss the blankets piled in the backyard, taking naps in the silver maple's shade. Peanut butter sandwiches on colorful plastic plates with ants jostling for crumbs. In these moments my desires were few: a little longer with the earth, for mosquitoes to fly past me entirely, please. I miss the aloneness you're only given as a child, without the expectation of anything greater. Take me there, to the sun-bleached yard and cricket songs. I will embrace my own self by the shoulders and squeeze. Say, like a soothsayer driven mad by the truth, *You must remember how this feels.* Someday, you will be halfway through your twenties. Forty hours of minimum wage work and then more—dishes, laundry, full grocery list behind a magnet. You will want to jump from the window with gusto—*Abandon life!* your inner voice cajoles—but this will be what saves you. This memory of twigs breaking beneath your body. Your grandmother's voice, *Alive! Alive!*, calling you back inside.

## THE MOVEABLE FUTURE

It's all irreversible. Every second. That one.
And this one too. I can't take any of it back.
Does it frighten you—how we move forward
even when we're delirious with boredom?
As you sleep, you're pulled further away from
birth, from the last moment you were held.
What waits for you in the moveable future? Nobody
knows, not even your gods. I can't recall the last time
I kissed my sister on the cheek, or if I told my father
that I loved him during our final phone call. Gone,
and what does it matter? All you can do with a memory
is remember it. Maybe fifty years from now they'll have
invented a machine that makes time malleable. I'll be reachable
from every hour of my life, at the bottom of every grave
I dug. Press a button and poof! Reverse the pain back
into naivety. Reverse the naivety back into my body.
I will hold my breath and, with it, my regrets. Each one
magicked into putty in my hands. But no, of course
that could never work. Because my life is irreversible
I've had no choice but to appreciate it as it's happening.
Damned details keeping me afloat against my will.
Like the cardinal returning to my window every spring.
The egg and cheese sandwich from the local market.
The airplane flying over my apartment, full of people
going home.

## NIGHT WALK

Past the car dealership dressed in debris and the hall
of tree limbs reaching for my heart, I walk along the edge of the road.
No sidewalks in my hometown so I follow the white line—
it could go on forever but I know it won't.
Eventually I'd hit the Niagara River. Reborn, or so the tourists would say.
My therapist told me to take walks when I feel anxious.
I've been thinking in confused circles again.
Mothers and fathers, lovers and selves. Where does one version of
myself end and another begin? I stand for a moment, off course and
straddling the broken middle of the street. The moon is a spotlight
and I'm caught in its heat. Maybe all is not lost after all.
Here, the past yields beneath my feet and the coyote are asleep
in the forest with their young. And I...I am walking away
from my own character study. I'm not sure who I am

but this will not be the thing that ends me.

## DAWN

Before bed, in our basement apartment, Dad and I recite our nightly prayers. We bless every member of our families, wish for morning and good dreams. After the door closes, I ask god for a sign and nothing happens. I ask god for a sign and now I am an adult spinning out on the icy highway. It's all slow-motion—the seatbelt digging at my chest, the unfinished sonnet tucked in my biology textbook—and I ask god to save my life because there's no one else to talk to. The guardrail is missing on this part of the road and I think this must be what I've been waiting for all these long years. If there was ever a sign telling me that I am all alone, this is it. A prayer, after all, is just a conversation with your future self. On the shoulder of the road, having narrowly avoided collision with a Nissan, I hear my younger self echoing an echo. She blesses her mother and her father. Every future lover. She repeats the lines she's fed and, once in darkness, turns to the pillowcase. She asks god if she will ever be happy and I slam my frozen palms against the steering wheel, icicle tears hanging from our nose.

Sweet girl, can you hear me now?

I love you.

I love you!

I will keep you alive until morning.

# FINAL BOWS

## I TURN ON THE GHOST LIGHT

even though I'm probably the most haunted thing in any crowd. Even though, admittedly, I'd love for a spectral figure to walk through my torso and remind me that I'm still alive. I turn on the ghost light and face away from its glow, the lamp casting a halo around my body. I stare into the darkness, opening a hole into my past, big enough to climb through.

Every evening, once I'm          finally alone, I make this
journey just to take a          peek at my old bedroom,
heavily postered and          water damaged and
mine. My bedroom,          where THE MOTHER
only halfway-painted          the ceiling, and THE
FATHER built          bookshelves from
plywood, and THE          LOVER curled an arm
around my waist, and THE          SELF learned their lines.

It would be easy to          stay here. Relive my
childhood and make          better choices, speak up
when prompted, tell          everyone that I loved
them—often and          with conviction.

But I don't want to be performing my whole life. I've already wasted so much time pretending.

I get down on my knees and kiss the carpet, then the walls, then the doorknob. Walk carefully back to the hole I made in the middle of my life and begin to cry over the ghost light still burning. Even in this lonesome season, I made sure I could find my way home.

# NOTES

"Double Jeopardy" is indebted to the late Alex Trebek, host of *Jeopardy!*, who my late father watched every evening without fail.

"Portrait of My Father as a Young Man" is written after Rainer Maria Rilke's poem of the same title.

An early version of "Genesis" had a previous home with *Olney Magazine* in 2023.

"Would It Have Killed You to Call Me Pretty Instead?" takes its title from Lucy Dacus's song "Brando."

"Lover's Fermentation" was published under a different title with *Anti-Heroin Chic* in 2022.

"Night Walk" is written after Franz Wright's poem of the same title.

## ACKNOWLEDGMENTS

Thank you to everyone at Central Avenue Poetry and Simon & Schuster that helped bring this project to life. Michelle, thank you for being so enthusiastic about my work. Jessica, thank you for your notes about THE SELF's role in this show, which were instrumental as I shaped this manuscript. Beau, thank you for your edits and formatting help, both of which I worried about for absolutely no reason. Molly, thank you for making sure I didn't have any embarrassing grammatical issues.

Thank you to Lyd Havens, my first editor, and the first person to read this collection in its entirety. Your advice (especially on em dashes, commas, and the formatting of "There's This Story She Tells") was incredibly helpful, as well as your encouragement.

Thank you to Sierra DeMulder, Kelly Grace Thomas, and Topaz Winters for penning such beautiful, touching blurbs for this collection. It is an honor to write with and know all of you.

Thank you to the staff of I Love Books in Delmar, New York (Melissa, Katie, Pam, Jen, Hannah F, Hannah S, and Abby) for being both wonderful coworkers and wonderful friends. You sell my book much better than I do!

Thank you to Ari, Clara, and Kayla, for being my readers, my workshop group, my everything. The idea for this collection was born in Vancouver, all of us together, when I admitted that I always felt like I was performing. Thanks for helping me tear the curtain down.

& thank you, as always, to Paul. My lover, number one in a million. I love you. Every performance is yours.